Phillip R. Greaves, 2ND

A GOVERNMENT OF SERVICE TO ALL

A Free Country For a Free People*

Copyright © 2010

All Rights Reserved

It is not the purpose of the law to provide a livelihood for attorneys, judges, administrators, or legislators. These are just side effects of the law. Its real purpose is to provide a framework for the peaceful interaction and coexistence of men and women within a common social structure. This purpose is most efficiently achieved when all citizens are fully informed of the content and effect of the law.

4   A Government of Service to All   4

4   A Free Country for a Free People   4

Other Books by
Phillip R. Greaves, 2nd

Society, Reason, Sexuality • Our Fountains of Pleasure, Truth and Order • 4 Your Consideration • The Power and Virtue of Lust • The Grand Delusion • A Government of Service to All • Water and Oil: Religion and Sex • Water and Oil: Sex and Government • Water and Oil: Government and Religion

Contents

8   A Government of Service to All   8

8   A Free Country for a Free People   8

ONE EQUALS INFINITY

The statement one equals infinity is not intended as a mathematical formula, or as a description of the universe, though it applies (the infinity of the one universe). No, this statement is meant as a political description stating the proper relationship between any individual and the masses in a free society.

The actual meaning of one equals infinity is this: the rights of men are not accumulative, men do not acquire any greater degree of their fundamental rights by joining together into groups or mobs. A collection of men has no more authority or primary rights than those held by an individual alone.

***

This is not the end of democracy, however. Democracy will continue to operate as it always has: as a decider of issues, and the ranking of men/women. We will still have to vote for the issues and vote for the workers, the President, Congress, etc. But changing the Constitution should be even harder than it now is. I suggest a four-fifths vote to add an amendment and the placing of certain provisions beyond even the vote of the people, least it become too easy to lose those hard-earned rights.

What will change, however, is that there shall no longer exist an eminent domain authority. Instead, there shall be a fine, against the government, of seven times the value of anything commandeered, to be paid to the individual from whom anything was unlawfully taken.

No individual will ever again be forced to surrender their lawfully held possessions, to any authority or group, except as a penalty for the unlawful violation of another's fundamental rights. Under such a system, taxation shall be phased-out and ended. Within a system of true equality, government shall be funded through voluntary means such as use and service fees, donations, and games of chance.

Instead of property taxes, there shall be a general, municipal, use and service fee that will be applied to all the uses property taxes were once applied to (except for the fire department, which should be funded by all homeowner's insurance companies operating within a given city or town), the non payment of which may result in a lien against the property of any noncompliant resident or property holder.

Such a lien may be levied against any and all properties owned by an individual, or business entity, for the non-payment of the GMUASF, but no confiscation of property may occur until the amount owed equals at least seventy-five percent of the full value of said properties.

The rationale for the GMUASF is pretty straightforward and obvious. Certain aspects of living in a community, which benefit all a city's citizens and residents, are simply better and more efficient when planned, maintained and administered by the local, municipal authority.

Some examples include roads and highways, parks, public schools, law enforcement, jails and prisons. There are several additional constraints on the GMUASF with regard to who will be required to pay it and how it will be calculated.

First, no one under the age of twenty-one shall be compelled to pay this charge, so that the youngest wage earners may enjoy their full income and accumulate some savings prior to assuming the full responsibilities of adulthood and citizenship.

Second, no one earning less than twenty thousand dollars per year shall be called upon to pay this fee, regardless of their age, as their income should be exempt from any mandatory expense being added to their cost of living.

Third, the GMUASF shall be no greater than one third of the estimated annual city budget divided equally among all city residents over the age of twenty-one with an income greater than twenty thousand dollars per year. Toward this end, there shall be a yearly census taken to determine who shall be charged this expense in the following year and how much they will be required to pay.

Fourth, those that are required to pay this use and service fee will have four options for doing so, annually, semi-annually, quarterly, or monthly.

Fifth, anyone paying the GMUASF who fails to earn the requisite twenty thousand plus dollars, in a given year, may demand a refund of all moneys they have paid in for that year in the beginning of the following year.

Sixth, in any year that the revenue from the GMUASF exceeds one third of the estimated annual city budget, said overage shall be equally divided and returned to all those that paid into it. If there is anything remaining above this division, it must be placed in a savings account to earn interest, which the government can take as revenue and keep.

The principle, however, must be returned to the next dispersal. The obligation to return such excesses to those who contributed to them may not be mitigated or suspended by either the legislature or the general populace. Any person that wishes his share left for the use of the legislature may donate it back after receiving it.

***

It is a long-standing position of the legal establishment that ignorance of the law is no excuse. This position was originally based on the belief that the law should be a matter of common sense, easily discernable with just a little reflection. So laws such as those against murder, rape, theft, trespassing, etc. required little in the way of mental effort or education to conceive and understand. Matters are not so simple today.

The law has become an enormous and complex subject requiring a great deal of education, discipline, and effort to comprehend and apply. Under such circumstances, ignorance of the law can only continue to be dismissed if the law is made readily and equally available to all. This is not the situation that exists today.

It is not the purpose of the law to provide a livelihood for attorneys, judges, administrators, or legislators. These are just side effects of the law. Its real purpose is to provide a framework for the peaceful inter-action and coexistence of men and women within a common social structure. This purpose is most efficiently achieved when all citizens are fully informed of the content and effect of the law.

Two ancient examples illustrate this position: Hammurabi, the greatest ruler of ancient Babylonia (1792-1750 B.C.E.), is best known for his code of laws, which he posted throughout his kingdom, so none would be ignorant of his decrees; and the Hebrew nation's requirement that male children memorize the Torah, which includes the law of Moses, prior to their thirteenth birthday and bar mitzvah (coming of age ceremony).

Such solutions as memorization or posting our laws in the town square, for all to see, are no longer practical. The complete laws of our land are too numerous to be memorized by any person, and they are too frequently changed, and added to, for a permanent display to be efficient. However, this does not mean the populace must go largely uninformed regarding the law.

No, there is an effective way to provide every citizen with an up-to-date copy of the laws that govern the common person, and a way to make specialty laws available to those they apply to. A general law book can, and should, be provided from each level of government to every resident and citizen, on an annual basis[1].

The telephone companies do this and our governments can too. It's the right thing for any government to do. No person should have to go to some high-priced lawyer, or his seat of government, just to become informed of the law. The legal system should bring the laws to every individual.

***

It is a national tragedy that the United States,

---

[1]   Alternately, and more economically, these rules and regulations could be uploaded to the internet where they would be readily available for anyone to print out at their own expense.

the nation that considers itself the freest in the world, now imprisons more of its citizens than any other country on Earth. This shame is caused by two aspects of the legal system, with regard to our laws and our treatment of criminals.

Our prison sentences are often of excessive duration and over fifty percent of the people serving them are there because of the war on drugs. These two factors have propelled our system of prisons and corrections into a rapid growth endeavor and, in some cases, a private enterprise.

The longer people are kept in a prison, the faster the space runs out, and the more people put behind bars, the quicker the need to build more correctional facilities. Don't misunderstand, murderers should be executed within ten years of their convictions. However, many other prisoners are given excessive sentences.

Many people imprisoned for drug offenses are sentenced to thirty, forty, fifty or more years. This is ridiculous. Such people shouldn't be in custody at all. Any individual should have the sovereign right to control their own body, and that includes what they may put in their body, and what substances they may choose for recreation.

Other criminals are also given extreme sentences that reflect a public desire for revenge[2], rather then a need to safeguard the

---

[2]   Sex offenders fall into this category and,

community or reform the transgressor. Such overly lengthy prison terms serve no legitimate purpose, inhibit reform, promote dependency, and prolong the public's burden

---

depending on whom you ask, are either the most, or the least, likely to re-offend. Where they are most likely to be repeat offenders, it is because there are no effective programs to help them reform, redirect, and reorient their sex drives, or to augment these efforts with masturbation. Prison administrators and personnel are generally hostile toward inmate masturbation, which results in an abnormally high level of aggression within most correctional facilities.

and expense.

A workable solution would be to limit prison terms to a maximum of ten years per incarceration. If a criminal is sentenced to a term of less than a decade, and afterwards is found guilty of additional crimes, their term of imprisonment may be raised to as much as the ten year limit. Under no circumstances, however, may any prisoner be sentenced to more than the ten-year limit, per internment in any correctional facility.

Such a solution would greatly reduce the public's burden and expense, and promote reform and independence following a prisoner's release back into the general populace. This limitation would only apply to terms of imprisonment.

Financial obligations, however, may be imposed without such limitation, per each crime an individual commits. Such monetary compensation may be collected either by confiscating a criminal's property or by garnisheeing their income, after their release from prison.

Only a garnishment of fifteen percent may be made against any person's income, and that must be evenly divided among all claimants until each is paid in full, regardless of how long this may take, or until the offender shall die.

This correctional strategy is to be applied to every criminal and every crime, except for murderers and murder, regardless of the emotional magnitude of the crime. So, thieves, conmen, counterfeiters, robbers, spouse-beaters, rapists, kidnappers and child-molesters[3] will all be treated according to this plan.

Many people, reacting emotionally, will

---

[3]   The most despised offender is the pedophile or "child-molester," as society tries to protect juveniles from the "corruption of sex." This extreme hatred of "child-molesting-pedophiles" is misdirected, due to the media's misrepresentations and its failure to distinguish between the pedosexual-pedophile (child-lover) and the pedo-cidal-psychopath (child-killer). So most people confuse one with the other, believing that pedophiles are child-rapists and murderers. This, of course, is untrue. From the way people react, one would think being sexually molested, or even raped, is the worst thing that could possibly happen to a child. Well, I can think of a few other things that are easily worse, like losing the use of an eye, hand, or leg, being paralyzed, suffering brain damage, being disfigured, etc. I would much rather be sexually "abused" then to have any of these other things inflected on me.

be angered that rapists, kidnappers and child-molesters[4] would receive no more than a ten-year-sentence, but they should consider the issue logically.

Instead of moaning that the sentences should be longer, or death, they should consider the effect that death and life sentences have on the victims. Would they rather have survivors of these crimes, or corpses? The problem goes all the way back to the Bible. If you're going to be stoned to death for using the "Lord's" name in vain why shouldn't you also disrespect your parents,

---

[4]   In 2008CE, the Supreme Court of the United States issued a ruling that child-rapists may not be sentenced to the death penalty unless their actions resulted in the death of their victim(s), as this would be cruel and unusual punishment.

commit fornication, adultery, rape, kidnapping, murder, etc.

After all, you're going to die anyway, and you can only be killed once. A death sentence is a death sentence, a life sentence is a death sentence too, because you're going to die in prison ether way.

The eighth amendment to the United States Constitution states, in part, "Excessive bail shall not be required, nor excessive fines imposed,..." Yet the reality of our present judicial system is that excessive bail is often required and excessive fines are routinely imposed, but this is treated as a mere difference of opinion between the justice system and the accused.

With regard to the justice system,

excessive bail and fines are those in excess of the magnitude of the crime and are compared to the bails and fines set for a particular crime throughout the country.

The legal system views both bails and fines as a means to fund the judiciary and prevent the flight of the accused. In certain cases, such as murder, bail is intentionally set so high that it is extremely unlikely that the defendant will be able to post it. At other times, bail is flat-out denied.

Our eighth amendment, however, was not written and added to the United States Constitution in order to empower the justice system, but to protect the rights of the accused. With this intent, the issue of what is excessive revolves around the resources of the defendant.

This means that bails and fines[5] are excessive whenever they exceed what the accused can afford, above his established financial commitments: such as food, housing, utilities, medications, and existing loans. The rational approach would be to require proof of a defendant's resources, prior to setting any bail or fine, and then to

---

[5]   The court would do well to note that these abusive penalties punish/harm more than just those convicted. Such excessive demands for money also hurt the defendant's family, taking the food from its children's mouths, as well as its landlord, utility providers, insurance agencies, and each of the convict's loan holders. In short, such fines hurt our general economy.

set such accordingly and fairly.

Our right not to testify against ourselves is acknowledged in the fifth Amendment to the USC[6]. Here also the court has twisted the meaning of the law, so that it not only protects us from any demand that we incriminate ourselves, but also prohibits us from testifying in our favor.

This is a travesty of justice. To be withheld from baring witness in our favor is

---

[6]   The fifth Amendment does not say that you can only avoid incrimination by remaining silent. Silence can incriminate one as easily as a confession. Necessarily then, this prerogative must include the right of a defendant to lie on the stand without threat of penalty. A defendant, therefore, should never swear any oath to tell the truth, as this actually negates one's right to avoid self-incrimination.

to be compelled to bare witness against ourselves. To say nothing in one's favor is to legitimize everything said against one.

Surly, the most amazing amendment to the USC[7] is clearly the fourteenth, which grants, to every citizen of the United States, the same rights and immunities under Federal law and equal protection of the law within every state. Its only real failing is that it only guarantees the right to vote to males over the age of twenty-one. That is why the nineteenth amendment was necessary to guarantee women the right to vote.

The fourteenth, however, did not deny the right to vote to either women or those

---

[7]   United States Constitution

under the age of twenty-one, but rather left this up to the states, as does the twenty-sixth with regard to those under the age of eighteen.

Furthermore, if taken literally, the fourteenth amendment also eliminates the age and residency restrictions, in the main body of the national constitution, regarding who can legally run for office, including the Presidency of the United States. Now it is not only native-born Americans that can run for the highest office, but naturalized citizens as well.

One cannot have equal protection of the laws without having the same laws applied to everyone. Therefore, if, in any state, a woman has the legal right to marry a consenting man, so too must a man have the legal right to marry a man, and the same goes for a man marrying a woman and a woman marrying a woman.

Calling gay marriage something other than marriage is just that old "separate but equal" scam that was tried on blacks not too many years ago. This doesn't mean, however, that any church or faith should be required to perform or accept gay marriages, but any that wish to certainly may. The only person who should be drafted to perform gay marriages is the Justice of the Peace. If he can't handle that part of the job, then he should resign.

Also, if a heterosexual couple has the right to adopt, in any state, so too must a homosexual couple have that right. Private adoption agencies and orphanages must be allowed to discriminate, however, if we are to be true to the one equals infinity position that the rights of the one are equal to the rights of the many.

***

When convicted criminals enter our jails and prisons and become wards of the state, they retain many of their civil rights, but not their civil liberties. They retain the right to legal counsel, the right to communicate with the outside world, the right to receive visitors, and the right to religious worship and practice.

Among the things they lose, however, are their freedom of motion, their independence, privacy, freedom of choice, some of their dignity, and most of all their ability to participate in the political life of our nation[8]. Convicts are not allowed to run for office or even vote (in some states). The rationale behind these political restrictions is to prevent the prison population from having any direct effect on the laws and conditions related to their incarceration.

Such a goal is misguided, at best. In any democracy, the prison population is simply too small to make a significant impact in the electorate with respect to any particular issue or candidate. Furthermore, the prison

---

[8]   Although I favor allowing prisoners the right to vote in public elections, I fully support the ban against their running for public office while they are in jail or prison, for obvious reasons.

population is no more likely to vote as a unified block than is the general populace.

On the positive side, allowing prisoners to vote would encourage them to see themselves as still part of the greater community (which they are), and to interact with it in a peaceful and rational way. It may even help them to reintegrate into society when their release comes due.

**

In ancient times, thirteen-year-olds were considered to be men and permitted to sit at the counsel of men and other tribal meetings. In the United States of America, the age of consent varies from thirteen to nineteen, but only those over eighteen are allowed voting rights throughout. California has voted on two occasions (so far) to give voting rights to sixteen-year-olds. The issue failed on both attempts, but the fact that the measure made it to the ballot (twice) shows that the subject actually had quite a lot of support.

Many people think that the twenty-sixth amendment to the United States' Constitution establishes the minimum voting age for the whole country, this is not correct. While the twenty-sixth amendment does require eighteen-year-olds be given the vote everywhere, it doesn't prohibit the states from allowing even younger citizens the right to vote. My own position on this matter is two fold. First, anyone, of any age, who serves in our military, should automatically have the right to vote in our elections.

Second, there should be a citizenship test where anyone who passes will be given full citizenship rights, including the right to vote and engage, as an adult, in consensual sexual activity, along with drug and alcohol consumption. This test should be open to everyone from five to twenty. No one who hasn't achieved adulthood, by growth or by test, should ever be tried as an adult in court.

***

The government should be allowed to compete with the private sector in any endeavor it may choose, provided that any such enterprises be started, funded, operated and maintained by voluntary means, to include free-market sales and purchase, contest, lotteries, donations, etc.

Originally, the purpose of Social Security was to provide an allowance for the retired, the aged, and single mothers. There is no reason why this program cannot be continued, but it must become a voluntary program funded by voluntary means. Later, Social Security was expanded to include health care through Medicare and Medicaid. These programs can also be continued under a voluntary format.

A great deal of money can be saved for these programs if the government would stop paying above market value for medical equipment. Our government's medical programs often pay double or more for the same items that cost half as much or less on the open market. A box of latex gloves, for example, cost around seven dollars in the private sector, but Medicare pays over fourteen dollars for the same item.

***

There is a very old, but underhanded and dishonest business practice that must be ended. I am speaking of the use of fine print on contracts and advertisements. The only reason that fine print is employed is to hide important information where the vision-impaired and careless will not see it.

While it's true that prices may go up, temporarily, the benefit to consumers will be enormous, as they will be more thoroughly informed with regard to their choices in the marketplace.

I think all businesses, licensed within

the USC, should be prohibited from using any print smaller than a twelve-point font on all contracts, advertisements and promotions after a given date.

There should be a hefty fine for any breach of this law. The only exception to this rule should be for advertisements and contracts that are printed in only one font size.

TAX-FREE AMERICA

Our forefathers made one mistake. What they should have fought for was representation without taxation.

--Fletcher Knebel

And you're working for no one but me.

(The Beatles, "Taxman")

EVERYONE HAS HEARD THE OLD SAYING, "...nothing is certain but death and taxes.[9]" This statement, while certainly true of death, is mistaken regarding taxes. There are many ways to avoid taxes. If you want to avoid sales tax on certain items (such as food, labor or clothing), there are sates you can move to where these items are not taxed. If you want to avoid state income tax, there are also states which do not tax income. Our federal government even allows certain tax-breaks to the chosen few who qualify.

But, if you want to avoid taxes

---

[9]   This well known saying comes to us from the last line of a quote of Benjamin Franklin.

altogether you have only two choices. One choice is to do all your business with unlicensed businesses and individuals which claim no income or property. Such businesses and persons neither collect nor surrender taxes. Your other choice for avoiding taxes is to support and promote voluntarily funded government[10] This means fighting for the right to keep and control your own money.

The black market has two major advantages over voluntarily funded government: It is already here, and nearly everyone uses it. Every time anyone sells something to a friend or a stranger, and fails to declare the

---

[10]   The possibility of voluntarily funded government is examined in the fifteenth chapter of "The Virtue Of Selfishness," by the late philosophical giant Ayn Rand.

income, collect or surrender taxes, they are part of the black market. The black market, however, has many very real dangers. Among these dangers are real criminals hiding from the law and trading illegal goods and services. Murderers, rapists, thieves, and conmen hide and do business on the black market alongside the otherwise honest tax-dodger.

Furthermore, governments believe they have a right to a part of everyone's income and property without regard for anyone's personal consent. For these reasons governments have declared the black market illegal. If you are caught doing business on the black market, the government may legally take all of your property, and/or imprison you. If you resist arrest, you may be shot and killed. If you want to avoid the dangers of the black market, and still escape taxation, your best choice is to support and promote voluntarily funded government.

Under voluntarily funded government you decide when, if and how much of your money goes for the support of government. As long as you respect the property rights of others, the government may not claim any part of your property without your uncoerced agreement.

There are two main problems with voluntarily funded government, however: It is not currently available, and it has never been tried. Because it has never been tried, many are at a loss as to how voluntarily funded government might work. After all,

who would just give money to the government?

***

Every day millions of us make promises and
commitments to others and depend on the
promises and agreements others make with
us. These promises and commitments are
contracts -- verbal and written -- relating to
everything from marriage vows to the
exchange of goods and services. The court
system exists, in part, to make sure these
promises are kept. Currently, the expense of
our court system is paid for by taxes and
fines. Under contract insurance, fines may
continue to pay for part of court system
expenses. Taxes, however, would be replaced
by optional contract insurance.

With contract insurance, our government would only protect those contracts which had been insured by the payment of a premium in the amount of a legally fixed percentage of the sums involved in the contract. This insurance would be voluntary, there would be no punishment for those who failed to buy it -- they would be free to make verbal agreements or sign uninsured contracts, if they choose.

Such contracts, however, would not be legally enforceable. If an uninsured contract were broken, the injured party would have to accept their losses -- their only recourse would be to spread a bad word and refuse to do future business with the contract breaker(s).

At this point, it must be understood that contract insurance need not require our government to make good on any of the contracts it insures, except for its own. Our government need only insure the right to a fair trail to determine the guilt and responsibility of the contract breaker(s). When awards are granted to the victim(s), our government may either award the victim(s) and require reimbursement from the guilty, or require direct payment by the guilty to the victim(s).

With regard to contracts of a more personal nature, such as marriage vows, an escape clause could be included or assumed (if omitted or excluded) to limit the responsibility of any party choosing to void the contract.

In most cases, however, voluntary contract insurance would work like a sales tax. Many of us would routinely insure the quality of products such as food, clothing, etc. by choosing to pay the contract insurance fee. In addition, optional contract insurance could even be used to insure foreign contracts, goods and services. This, in turn, would add foreign moneys to the support of our court system -- reducing its cost to us.

The vast majority of all contracts are fulfilled without any recourse to the courts. Revenue resulting from contract insurance fees would, therefore, greatly surpass the needs of the court system. This excess revenue could be applied to the funding of all other governmental services. The largest share of this revenue would come from the most productive and wealthiest individuals and businesses. This is as it should be because these have the greatest values to protect and, therefore, the most to lose from broken contracts.

It should now be obvious that this form of voluntarily funding government could easily fund all necessary government services at a rate of under ten percent per contract. The revenue generated could be split among city, county, state and federal agencies to cover every level of governmental service.

***

Another method for voluntarily funding the government would be a national lottery. Such a lottery already exists in many foreign countries and several of our own States also hold lotteries. These lotteries bring in enormous sums of money -- both monthly and annually.

Such lotteries have never been used to eliminate taxes, but there is no real reason why they couldn't or shouldn't. A national lottery could easily have several levels of winners ranging from a few dollars to, perhaps, a billion.

As with optional contract insurance, a national lottery could be open to foreign players, adding foreign moneys to the support of our government. Government's share of lottery proceeds could be used to support governmental agencies and services at all levels -- that is, local, county, state, and federal.

Just as optional contract insurance would draw most of its revenue from the rich and upper-middle-class, so a national lottery would draw most of its revenue from the poor and lower-middle-class without causing any undue hardship among the lottery's participants. Such a lottery could be split among city, county, state and federal agencies to cover every level of governmental service.

Ideally, such a split would give the largest revenue shares to local and federal agencies because they have the smaller revenue base to draw from. The local agencies, however, should receive the largest share of revenue (collected in their area) as the most immediate areas of service.

Although such a lottery could support our government on its own, if it were used in addition to optional contract insurance it would guarantee the success of voluntarily funded government.

***

So far, I have mentioned two methods of voluntarily funding the government (optional contract insurance and a national lottery). I have explained how each would work and some of their benefits. Each of these methods is based on providing some benefit beyond funding government in general.

In the case of optional contract insurance, the direct benefit is the ability to sue contract breakers -- individuals, groups, organizations. The direct benefit of a national lottery is the chance to win a large jackpot or smaller prize. In both of these cases, funding our government by voluntary means is a secondary benefit. There is, however, a more direct, if more questionable, way to voluntarily fund our government. This would involve direct donations to our government for the sole purpose of funding its services and agencies.

To understand how funding our government by direct donations could work, consider the methods used to fund charities. Examples are many. Churches, for instance, pass around collection plates, hold fund-raisers, and even ask their supporters for special donations for many causes. Many churches are enormously successful at getting what they ask for. Other charities employ television, radio, mailings and door-to-door solicitors in their efforts to raise money for their many causes.

Many of these charities are extremely well funded. In all cases, however, the funding of these charities comes just for the asking. It should not be too difficult to foresee many of us routinely donating money to our government for the support of the military, the police force or the court system[11]. It is even easier to envision us

---

[11]   The only things worse than a tax supported police force, court system and/or governing body, are any which are financially dependent on criminal fines and penalties, as these represent a conflict of interest. When crime is

high, these generate large sums of money for such agencies, which they quickly become dependent on. Then, when crime abates, they suffer from a lack of revenue. Calls for higher taxes quickly follow to make-up for these shortfalls. Although fines and penalties may act to deter crime, when they are enforced, the only way to remove the conflict of interest, they create, is to disperse all these funds to non-governmental, non-religious, randomly selected, charities. As an alternative to taxes, penalties, and fines, governmental telethons might prove successful. Radiothons might also be employed for such purposes.

frequently sending donations to our government to support its many charities.

The fact that governmental funding through donation is not connected to providing any direct benefit to the donors (apart from funding our government), however, makes it the least likely method for funding our governments without taxes. Optional contract insurance and a national lottery are more likely to succeed in this purpose.

Nevertheless, direct donations to our government are an excellent way to fund its many charities and social programs. Donations are, in fact, the most moral method of funding our governments' charitable activities.

It should now be clear that it is possible to replace tax funded government with voluntarily funded government. This fact, however, raises three very important questions: (1)Why should voluntarily funded government be preferred over taxes? (2)If voluntarily funded government is so much better, why are we still being taxed? (3) How can the change from taxes to voluntarily funded government be brought about?

The reasons that voluntarily funded government should be preferred over taxation are both moral and practical. The wage earner, the businessman, the land owner all have an absolute right to the whole of their property -- having gained it through voluntary trade and being free persons. No one, not even a government, should be allowed to gain any part of their property except through the same method of voluntary trade.

***

Whatever is taken from its owner(s) without their consent is stolen. Taxes, because they are taken in this manner, are stolen property. A government has no more right to steal for an alleged public good than a robber has to steal for a favorite charity. When a government claims the right to steal, by what right can it punish others for doing the same?

The government that taxes commits robbery. Furthermore, an individual's property is its life. A government that claims a share of any individual's property, apart from their consent, enslaves them. A person who is taxed is not free. They are owned by the government taxing them.

Practical reasons for preferring voluntarily funded government to taxation relate to cost savings and putting the control of our government back into the hands of each and every one of us. The cost saving benefit of voluntarily funding government is fairly straight-forward. Eliminating taxes means eliminating tax returns and the cost and paperwork associated with them. This is no small benefit for the government or the rest of us.

Under our current tax system, the cost of tax refunds and the filing of tax returns consumes a large share of tax revenues and results in enormous governmental, corporate and personal headaches. What voluntarily funded government would produce in revenue, would be fully available for providing governmental services. The size, power and function of the IRS would be greatly changed and reduced.

The greatest practical benefit, however, would be the much improved ability to hold the government in check. Every individual, within a government's area of service, would be empowered to withhold their share of government's funding (except for the GMUASF) any time they discovered their government overstepping its bounds, infringing the rights of its clients, misusing the funding it receives or providing inadequate service relative to its level of support.

Individuals might also, rightfully and occasionally, apply their resources to a more urgently considered need or goal. The right of free persons to determine their share, of government's funding, should be recognized as an essential right, on par with freely electing their representatives.

All this raises the question of why we are still being taxed. After all, if voluntarily funded government is workable, achievable and clearly better, why are we still bearing the burden of taxes? The answers to this question are multiple and relate to tradition, the nature of government and corruption.

***

Taxes are the traditional means for funding government, going all the way back to the tribute demanded by tribal chiefs and kings as landlords and supreme rulers. Before the American Revolution, the government of every nation was headed by a king and/or queen who ruled over their people. The purpose of government was to command, control, direct, guide and manage its people.

People were the wards, servants, and often the slaves of the kings. Private property was nonexistent. A king owned both the land and his people. Whatever possessions his people held, they held by the king's permission. The American Revolution radically changed the very nature of government.

America's   founding   fathers   viewed

government as our servant -- the exact opposite of the traditional view. They saw the individuals among us as sovereign, with fundamental and irrevocable rights. America's founding fathers held that the purpose of government was to protect and defend the rights of individuals (within a government's area of service) from any violation of their rights by other individuals, groups or governments. For this purpose, America's Founders created a representative government, "...of the people, by the people, and for the people."

So radical and so great were the achievements of our founders in creating a fundamentally new kind of government that they should not be greatly blamed for failing to

establish a voluntarily funded one -- espec-
ially considering that the constitution they
wrote provides the means to correct this
mistake. Nevertheless, taxes are a flaw cor-
rupting the great American experiment of a
free country for a free people.

The worst mistake (the one which keeps
the others in place) America's founding
fathers made was calling the thing they
created government. The word government
belongs to the enemies of freedom.

***

Government comes from the Greek word
meaning to steer or guide. To steer or guide is
to control, direct and manage. (You steer a
horse, you steer a car, you don't steer a man).
This is the old definition of government.

***

It is very difficult to change the definition of a word. It is much easier, more effective and more efficient to create a new word, or to use a short description. If America's founding fathers had called their creation a national security service, most of their other mistakes would already have been corrected. A national security service lacks the parental air of a government.

Without the parental air of authority, American freedom would have already reached its full and proper growth. Americans (and many others) would now enjoy the maximum level of personal freedom allowed by reason, fairness and justice. Serious crime would be the rarest of things.

Government's parental air, however, can only be maintained through taxation. Without compulsory funding (taxes), our government would either have collapsed or surrendered the last of its parental authority long ago.

The combination of a parental attitude and taxation, however, have led to an enormous failure for the experiment in freedom. Instead of a national security service, dedicated to the growth and security of rational, individual rights; we have a parental government directing all of us for the alleged good of the national family. So, here is the old government commanding each of us as to what we may or may not do, and how much of our money we may keep for ourselves.

Here we have the spectacle of elected representatives creating excuses (agencies, programs, wars, social objectives) to reach deeper and deeper into the pockets of individuals -- who may not refuse -- in order to impose order that is neither desired or needed, seeking to gain prestige that is not deserved.

***

A disdain for government's parental attitude, however, should not be viewed as a rejection of proper law and order. Proper law and order are essential to the security of any society. Without such order, individual freedom would be impossible.

The necessary limits of freedom and guidelines for proper law and order are described by two simple principles: (1)No individual, group or agency may violate the person or property of a non-consenting other. (2)Doing so requires the violator to forfeit values of comparable worth.

Anything beyond these two principles is oppression and tyranny. The purpose of law and order then is to protect each of us against any violation of our person or property, and to insure reparations (where appropriate) from any violator thereof.

***

Some of the primary reasons we are still burdened with taxes are that few of us are aware of the possibility of voluntarily funded government and our elected representatives are unwilling to surrender their ability to reach into our pockets at their convenience. This brings us to the question of how the change from taxes to voluntarily funded government can be achieved.

America's   change   from   taxes   to

voluntarily funding government cannot be achieved immediately. Before taxes can be eliminated, voluntarily funded government must first be established. Optional contract insurance, a national lottery and donations must be put into operation before taxation can be abandoned.

The security of our nation requires that government funding be continuous throughout the change from taxation to voluntarily funded government. The first step, therefore, is to educate everyone concerning the possibility of voluntarily funding government and to encourage them to notify their representatives of the demand for its creation and establishment.

NO MORE REGESTRATION

It has been over thirty years since then-President-Jimmy Carter pardoned the Vietnam area draft-dodgers, suspended military conscription and established the selective service system as an emergency, call-to-arms. Thus were America's all-volunteer-forces born, and served us well they have and do. And yet, our politicians refuse to put their complete trust in a military that isn't driven by the whip.

From its top brass to its greenest

private, almost no one, among today's troops, wants a return to the
days of compulsory service. Nearly
everyone acknowledges that a
volunteer makes a better, more loyal
and effective soldier than most any
man made to service his country by
force.

Furthermore, a drafted force is
an affront to the nation that demands one. A draft implies that the
citizenry is so apathetic toward, disgusted with, or oppressed by their
politicians, they'd rather be overrun

by an invading force than defend their homes. This has never been a problem within the United States.

Although the United States has often employed the use of con-scription, it has never actually needed to. Her citizens have always stood ready to defend their home-land and the principles upon which their nation has been founded. Although ignored and denied, these very principles, as expressed in our Constitution's thirteenth amend-ment, demand that the use of a military draft, and any mandated registration for such, be permanently abandoned and abolished.

Composed and ratified, following America's civil war, the thirteenth amendment reads, **"Neither slavery nor involuntary servitude, except as a punishment for crime whereof the party shall have been duly convicted, shall exist within the United States, or any place subject to their jurisdiction."** To the best of my knowledge, it is not a crime to be male, eighteen or under the age of twenty-seven. Nor have I ever heard of anyone being convicted of these "offenses."

For those who would exempt mandatory service from the province of the thirteenth amendment, by referring to the general welfare clause of the Constitution's preamble, I will simply point out that amendments always override everything that precedes them in the event of a contradiction. Were it otherwise, do-gooders could claim that prohibition is still in effect because the amendment that created it came before the one that ended it.

Not being one to call for civil disobedience, I encourage everyone touched, or moved by this issue, to write their governor, and congressmen, urging them to do the right thing and have the instrument of the draft, and any registration related to such a device, officially and permanently, prohibited under any and all circumstances.

***

It has been long over due, and I join my brothers and sisters in their celebration. I only hope our jubilation is not premature. Allowing soldiers to openly claim their homosexuality, is one thing, actually permitting gay sexual behavior, in on post housing, or in town, is something else, altogether.

If it has not already been addressed and revised, the military code of justice needs to be modified to allow the sexual conduct that defines our kind and our culture. This code regulates every aspect of a soldier's life (on and off post) and prescribes penalties for any breach thereof. It even seeks to govern a soldier's sexual conduct.

When I served, heterosexuals were only allowed reproductive style intercourse, and everything that could be described as gay sex: sodomy, fellatio (sorry ladies no fun for you either, *and I can't find the spelling*) were prohibited and punishable. If this hasn't been changed, then it needs to be. Allowing sexual openness, while requiring celibacy is not acceptable.

Besides, many straight boys and girls like sodomy and oral sex too. Don't you? Yeah, you know it.

NOTHING BUT MARRIAGE

Don't let anyone fool you. Marriage is not a contract between those getting married and any state. Our governments should do nothing more than to perform these ceremonies, or to act as witness to these events. It should not have any voice in marriage apart from this. Government should not presume to select or approve the spouses to be.

Marriage is an agreement, between those marrying, to love, respect, and honor each other for the rest of their lives. It should not be viewed as a license to have children, nor a demand that one should. The traditional vows don't even mention having children or raising them.

It is not a right, purpose, or power of government to define or regulate marriage. Nor should any church be allowed to define or regulate marriage beyond their own membership. Certainly, not by force of law. There is no church that can rightfully claim a copyright on the institution of wedlock.

Society itself is not qualified to define the meaning or character of matrimony for any of the individuals of which it is formed. The rights of the many are never greater than the rights of the one. Marriage should be defined exclusively by those being married and those intending to marry.

The fourteenth amendment to our

national constitution (USC[12]), clearly states, in its first clause, "All persons born or naturalized in the United States, and subject to the jurisdiction thereof, are citizens of the United States and of the state wherein they reside. No state shall make or enforce any law which shall abridge the privileges or immunities of citizens of the United States: nor shall any state deprive any person of life, liberty, or property, without due process of law; nor deny to any person within its jurisdiction the equal protection of the laws."

Except for requiring that the States grant twenty-one-year-old males the right to vote (in its second clause), the fourteenth

---

[12]   United States' Constitution

amendment makes no distinction among citizens on the basis of class, gender, race, age, sexuality, wealth or political/religious affiliation.

No special rights for the rich or the poor, black or white, male or female, young or old, gay or straight. Everything a citizen is, one is. For each citizen is a citizen, and every citizenship is the same. No legal distinction among the Hindu, atheist, Jew, Christian, or agnostic.

I would think that our rights and immunities probably begin with those presented in the first ten amendments to our Federal Constitution, and every citizen is entitled to them. But these are the rights of individuals, institutions do not have rights.

Now the states are required to provide equal protection under the law, but equal protection can not be achieved unless the same law is applied to everyone. All states recognize a woman's right to marry a man and a man's right to marry a woman, but all citizens must have the same rights. Until men share with women the right to marry men, and until women share with men the right to marry women, all parties consenting, the genders will never achieve true political equality.

Recently, The Connecticut Supreme Court ruled that separate wasn't equal. Anything less than marriage violated equal protection laws. Homosexuals don't want any marriage equivalency status, passed by any state, chiefly because the rights granted by such an instrument wouldn't follow them from state to state as legally binding, nor would it have any effect on an individual's status under federal law. In sort, nothing but marriage will do. Besides, a word is not copyrightable. Its meaning is always open to change.

Also recently, California had an election to determine the status of gay marriage, as to whether or not the Californian government would continue to recognize such unions. A hoard of Mormons descended on California and stayed long enough to vote on the measure themselves. Rarely have I been so disgusted by these meddlesome, religious pricks and their continuous interference in matters that really do not concern them.

Gay marriage is not going to impose any obligations on them at all. Nothing will require any church to accept or perform gay marriages or weddings. The only person that will be drafted in this affair will be the Justice of the Peace. Only this office will be required to perform such services. The religious interference on this issue has only one real goal and that is to impose religious, "moral" values on the rest of us through political force, and this, above all else, should be illegal.

Once an amendment, defining the conditions, rights and liberties of citizenship has been passed (such as the fourteenth amendment to the USC), no common law, or amendment to any lesser constitution, should ever be entertained by any legislator, or presented to the public for a vote, regarding any aspect of the amendment in question, as it will automatically supersede and cancel any such effort.

No, an amendment can only rightfully be modified or replaced by a new amendment at the same governmental level (or higher). It is up to the judiciary to determine if a particular situation or circumstance falls under the authority of a given amendment and not an issue for the electorate to decide.

Sooner or later, I hope it's sooner, the issue of gay marriage will reach the Supreme Court of the United States. I am confident the highest court will rule in favor of gay marriage and the right of homosexuals to define marriage for themselves.

SINGLE GENDER FAMILES

The actual rearing of children is beyond the scope of this paper. What I would like to present, however, are the many ways by which homosexuals can become parents and the advantages and disadvantages of each.

Many people wrongly assume that because homosexuals are not sexually inclined toward the opposite sex, they have no interest in raising children. This is a very mistaken notion. Other people feel strongly that homosexuals set a bad example, and therefore, shouldn't be allowed to raise kids.

This prejudice is also in error. Once a child has come into such a family, gay parent(s) are fully able to do all the same things heterosexuals would do for the care and nurture of their children. But having children, in the first place, is a little more complicated for them.

Perhaps the easiest way for a homo-sexual to become a parent is to adopt the children of a lover who was previously part of a heterosexual union. It may be difficult, however, to find a potential mate with this qualification.

They would be a stepparent and might not receive much respect from their new brood. After all, such children already have a mom and dad, why would they want a stepparent at all? Before one could assume the position of well loved and respected stepfather/mother, they would have to make friends with the children first.

Another way for homosexuals to become parents would to engage in heterosexual intercourse strictly for the purpose of pro-creation. Arrangements regarding the custody of the pending child may be decided on the basis of the child's gender: a little girl would become the child of its lesbian mother and her spouse, while a boy would become the child of the gay couple that includes his sire.

There are other variations regarding this reproductive strategy. Instead of the sperm coming from a member of the gay couple, a different donor might be employed. Egg donors are also available. Additionally, there may well be fees to pay donor(s), surrogate(s) and doctor(s).

If it is important for the child to receive its genes from at least one member of a given couple, and heterosexual intercourse is considered undesirable, artificial insemination may be used instead. In any event, the health, condition and appearance of the pending child should be considered carefully.

Finally, a homosexual couple might opt for adoption. Adoption allows one to select the characteristics considered most important, and the aesthetics values too, as they are already expressed in a living child. The medical files are generally available on children awaiting families.

Unfortunately, many adoption agencies are unwilling to consider single-gender families. Fortunately, there are many agencies and some of them will consider gays as potential parents.

UNCONSTITUTIONAL

I can not speak with respect to the entire municipal ordinance under which we, the people of Pueblo, live but if the nuisance laws are any indication, things are pretty bad all over. At several points, within the nuisance ordinances, these laws are in direct violation of our National Constitution, as the supreme law of the land.

Our nuisance laws contain a provision allowing a code enforcer to identify and declare a nuisance, even if it is not enumerated within the text of the law. This is arbitrary, unfair and violates due process.

It's arbitrary because it depends entirely upon the whim of the inspecting officer, which makes it unfair, as the violation cannot be identified and avoided beforehand. This violates due process because such an offence rest upon the decree of an individual. Any other law would be debated in counsel (or in public) before being voted into law. It's so much more then this, though. The enforcer also has the power to abate said infractions, without giving the property owner any notice at all. The owner will soon get the bill.

Now the code enforcer becomes, not only jury, judge and executioner, but legislator, as well. When was the code enforcer ever elected to its position? This is a violation of our Nationally guarantied right to due process. Additionally, these ordinance violate a defendant's right to a jury trial as well as the court appointed attorney guaranteed to the poor.

There are no Constitutional grounds for denying anyone a trail by jury. Most certainly not because the Court has set a time limit on declaring one's prerogative. Nor because some municipal authority wants a twenty-five dollar jury fee. Both of these conditions are Constitutionally invalid.

Additionally, one's entitlement to Court appointed counsel does not depend on whether or not one faces a possible jail sentence. The only Constitutional restrictions on this provision are that one must be unable to afford an attorney on one's own and that the amount in dispute (one's fine, for example) be greater than twenty dollars.

Our Federal Constitution forbids excessive fines and bales. And, as the eighth amendment was added to the United States Constitution to protect the rights of the defendant, these involuntary expenses are excessive whenever they exceed the liquid assets of the accused minus their other obligations.

The court would do well to note that these abusive penalties punish/harm more than just the convicted. Such excessive demands for money also hurt the defendant's family, taking the food from its children's mouths, as well as its landlord, utility providers, insurance agencies, and each of the convict's loan holders. In short, such fines harm our general economy. Whatever is unconstitutional is also illegal.

The true purpose of the law is to provide a framework for the peaceful interaction and coexistence of men and women within a common social structure. It is a fact that this goal is most efficiently reached when every citizen/resident is fully informed of the content and effect of the law.

Pueblo has done a very poor job of getting these laws into hands of we common folk. It actually seems that the public authorities of this city don't really want the text of our laws in the hands of the people. Sure, they have a website which contains these laws, but it can be difficult to find them even after one finds the website.

Once you find them, you will also notice

how user unfriendly they are. To save you some unnecessary trouble, here is the full address to all our many laws and ordinance http://www.pueblo.us/cgi-bin/gt/tpl_page.html,template=1%26content=368%26nav1=1% 26 I strongly suggest that everyone printout (even if you have to go to the library to do so) a copy of these municipal laws, 'cause that's where all the loopholes are.

By all men call holy, such Constitutional abuses and due process violation may make our city a sitting duck for some eager lawyer to launch a very large class-action suit. This could cripple our economy. I'd really hate to see that happen, we all suffer too much all ready.

I also advise that advertising the

internet site of our laws be carried-out in the following manner: first, get all the television stations, operating locally, and the cable and dish companies, to advertise the complete address at lest three times a week, during peak hours. Second, include the newspaper for at least one prominent add spot per week.

The local radio stations should also share in this responsibility and announce the address at least three times a day, during prime broadcast hours. I'm certain you can get this done with the television and radio folks, as these must have their licenses renewed from time to time, from the good people down at City Hall.

LOCAL MAGISTRATE ERRS

The stunningly-attractive, silver-haired magistrate who boasts of authoring the woefully inadequate, meagerly-informative-pamphlets at our new, municipal, court house, is so in love with his own efforts that he is willfully blind to their shortcomings.

Indeed, he fails to give proper consideration to his presumed, public audience, the first rule of writing and communication in general. Surely, these pamphlets aren't intended for the consumption of lawyers or paralegals who are well informed of the language, content and context of the law.

It is not the purpose of the law to

provide a livelihood for attorneys, judges, administrators, or legislators. These are just side effects of the law. Its real purpose is to provide a framework for the peaceful interaction and coexistence of men and women within a common social structure. This purpose is most efficiently achieved when all citizens are fully informed of the content and effect of the law.

While the term arraignment is defined, in the court's pamphlets, as an individual's first appearance, a large segment of the population has only the vaguest idea of what this term means, which they generally got from such television shows as "Law and Order."

Furthermore, most people are going to

be ignorant of the terms and conditions, identified in these pamphlets, until their first court appearance, by which time it is too late (under Pueblo's municipal law) to request/demand a jury trail, or court appointed attorney. The Court uses these facts to railroad defendants and fleece the public.

It should be required that the accused be given these pamphlets with their first notice of any violation. I may be a bit naïve, but I know of no provision in our Federal Constitution (the supreme law of the land) allowing anyone to deny a defendant's demand for a jury trial for any reason, much less a failure to make such a demand in a "timely manner," before hand. A jury trail is a right of every defendant and a matter of their prerogative alone.

Additionally, the pamphlets state that a defendant's first appearance will be before the court, this is incorrect. There is a difference between making a plea in the courthouse and making it before the Court. One should rightfully expect to make one's plea before, at least, an officer of the court, which a mere clerk is not.

What is worse, however, is that these clerks pretend to be ignorant of the contents of Mr. Alexander's pamphlets and pur- posefully resist any request that might result in additional expense (such as a jury trail) for the court.